RV and Camping
Travel Log
and
Budget Book

Grace O. Kirby

First Printing: 2019

ISBN-13: 9781793950123

Grace O. Kirby
Massillon, Ohio 44646

Ordering Information:

Please go to our Facebook page to order.

https://www.facebook.com/RVCampingTravelLog/

RV and Camping
Travel Log
and
Budget Book

Emergency Info

Name____

Address____

City____

State________________________________Zip Code___________________

Phone____

Incase of an emergency please contact...

Name____

Address____

City____

State________________________________Zip Code___________________

Phone Number____

Or

Secondary contact..

Name____

Address____

City____

State________________________________Zip Code___________________

Phone Number____

Maps

For you to color in the state or provance you have been to.

United States of America

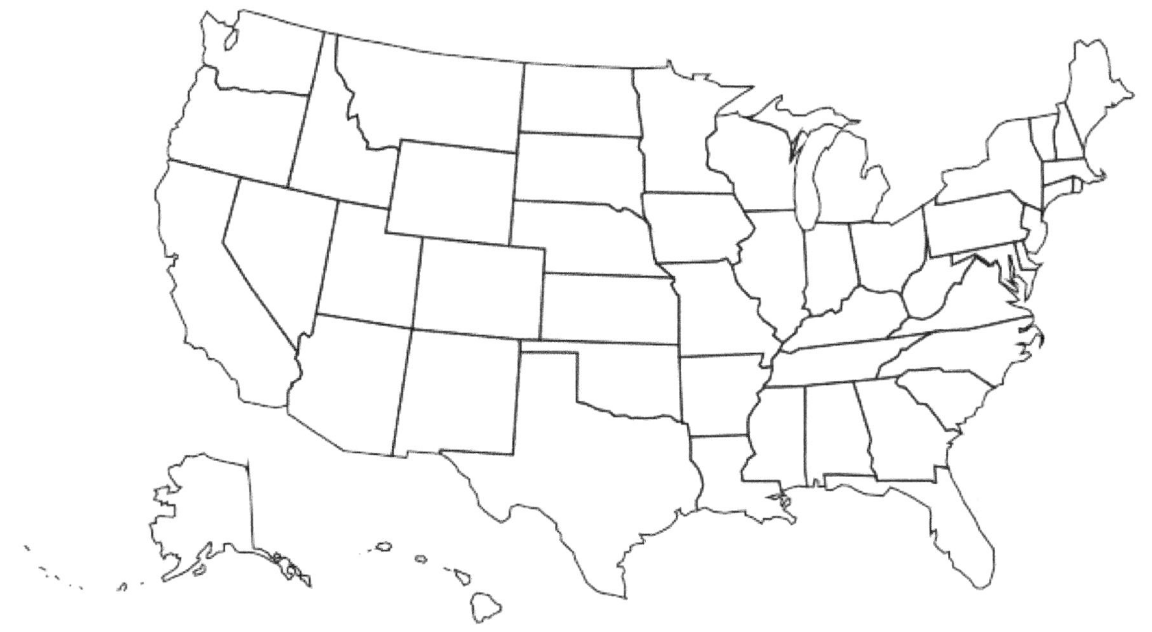

States we have gone to...

Alabama	Alaska	Arizonia	Arkansas	California
Colorado	Connecticut	Delaware	Florida	Georgia
Hawaii	Idaho	Illinois	Indiana	Iowa
Kansas	Kentucky	Louisiana	Maine	Maryland
Massachusetts	Michigian	Minnesota	Mississippi	Missouri
Montana	Nebraska	Nevada	New Hampshire	New Jersey
New Mexico	New York	North Carolina	North Dakota	Ohio
Oklahoma	Oregon	Pennsylvania	Rhode Island	South Carolina
South Dakota	Tenneessee	Texas	Utah	Vermont
Virginia	Washington	West Virginia	Wisconsin	Wyoming

Canada

Provances we have gone to...

Alberta		British Columbia		Labrador		Manitoba		New Brunswick
Newfoundland		Northwest Territory		Nova Scotia		Nunavut		Ontario
Prince Edward		Quebec		Saskatchewan		Yukon		

Mexico

States we have gone to...

Aguascalientes	Baja California	Baja California Sur	Campeche	Chiapas
Distrito Federal	Chihuahua	Coahuila	Colima	Durango
Guanajuato	Guerrero	Hidalgo	Jalisco	Mexico
Michoacan	Morelos	Nayarit	Nuevo Leon	Oaxaca
Puebla	Queretaro	Quintana Roo	San Luis Potosi	Sinaloa
Sonora	Tabasco	Tamaulipas	Tlaxcala	Veracruz
Yucatan	Zacatecas			

Month	**Campground List**						
Day	Campground Name	City	Cost	Rating	Cell Service	Day Limit	Comment
1							
2							
3							
4							
5							
6							
7							
8							
9							
10							
11							
12							
13							
14							
15							
16							
17							
18							
19							
20							
21							
22							
23							
24							
25							
26							
27							
28							
29							
30							
31							

Month

Monthly Income				
	Left from last month	Added	Spent	Balance
Retiredment Check				
Work Pay Check				
Youtube				
Amazon				
Etsy				
401K				
Other income 1				
Other income 2				
Other income 3				
Totals				

Fixed Expenses				
	Amount from last month	Added	Spent	Balance
Camper Payment				
Phone				
Internet				
Amazon				
Netflix				
Health Insureance				
Vehicle Insureance				
Post Office Box				
Totals				

Monthly Expenses											
Date	Gas	Propane	BlackTank	GreyTank	Water	Food	Laundry	Medical	Medication	Repairs		
1												
2												
3												
4												
5												
6												
7												
8												
9												
10												
11												
12												
13												
14												
15												
16												
17												
18												
19												
20												
21												
22												
23												
24												
25												
26												
27												
28												
29												
30												
31												
Total												

Other Monthly Expenses												
Date												
1												
2												
3												
4												
5												
6												
7												
8												
9												
10												
11												
12												
13												
14												
15												
16												
17												
18												
19												
20												
21												
22												
23												
24												
25												
26												
27												
28												
29												
30												
31												
Total												

Monthly Totals

	Balance From last month	Budgeted +/-	New Balance
Total from Campgrounds			
Total Fixed Expenses Page 1			
Total Fixed Expenses Page 2			
Gas			
Propane			
Black Tank			
Grey Tank			
Water			
Food			
Laundry			
Medical			
Medication			
Repairs			
Total			

Notes

Month	**Campground List**						
Day	Campground Name	City	Cost	Rating	Cell Service	Day Limit	Comment
1							
2							
3							
4							
5							
6							
7							
8							
9							
10							
11							
12							
13							
14							
15							
16							
17							
18							
19							
20							
21							
22							
23							
24							
25							
26							
27							
28							
29							
30							
31							

Month

Monthly Income

	Left from last month	Added	Spent	Balance
Retiredment Check				
Work Pay Check				
Youtube				
Amazon				
Etsy				
401K				
Other income 1				
Other income 2				
Other income 3				
Totals				

Fixed Expenses

	Amount from last month	Added	Spent	Balance
Camper Payment				
Phone				
Internet				
Amazon				
Netflix				
Health Insureance				
Vehicle Insureance				
Post Office Box				
Totals				

Date	Gas	Propane	BlackTank	GreyTank	Water	Food	Laundry	Medical	Medication	Repairs		
1												
2												
3												
4												
5												
6												
7												
8												
9												
10												
11												
12												
13												
14												
15												
16												
17												
18												
19												
20												
21												
22												
23												
24												
25												
26												
27												
28												
29												
30												
31												
Total												

Other Monthly Expenses												
Date												
1												
2												
3												
4												
5												
6												
7												
8												
9												
10												
11												
12												
13												
14												
15												
16												
17												
18												
19												
20												
21												
22												
23												
24												
25												
26												
27												
28												
29												
30												
31												
Total												

Monthly Totals

	Balance From last month	Budgeted +/-	New Balance
Total from Campgrounds			
Total Fixed Expenses Page 1			
Total Fixed Expenses Page 2			
Gas			
Propane			
Black Tank			
Grey Tank			
Water			
Food			
Laundry			
Medical			
Medication			
Repairs			
Total			

Notes

Month		**Campground List**					
Day	Campground Name	City	Cost	Rating	Cell Service	Day Limit	Comment
1							
2							
3							
4							
5							
6							
7							
8							
9							
10							
11							
12							
13							
14							
15							
16							
17							
18							
19							
20							
21							
22							
23							
24							
25							
26							
27							
28							
29							
30							
31							

Month

Monthly Income

	Left from last month	Added	Spent	Balance
Retiredment Check				
Work Pay Check				
Youtube				
Amazon				
Etsy				
401K				
Other income 1				
Other income 2				
Other income 3				
Totals				

Fixed Expenses

	Amount from last month	Added	Spent	Balance
Camper Payment				
Phone				
Internet				
Amazon				
Netflix				
Health Insureance				
Vehicle Insureance				
Post Office Box				
Totals				

Monthly Expenses												
Date	Gas	Propane	BlackTank	GreyTank	Water	Food	Laundry	Medical	Medication	Repairs		
1												
2												
3												
4												
5												
6												
7												
8												
9												
10												
11												
12												
13												
14												
15												
16												
17												
18												
19												
20												
21												
22												
23												
24												
25												
26												
27												
28												
29												
30												
31												
Total												

Other Monthly Expenses											
Date											
1											
2											
3											
4											
5											
6											
7											
8											
9											
10											
11											
12											
13											
14											
15											
16											
17											
18											
19											
20											
21											
22											
23											
24											
25											
26											
27											
28											
29											
30											
31											
Total											

Monthly Totals

	Balance From last month	Budgeted +/-	New Balance
Total from Campgrounds			
Total Fixed Expenses Page 1			
Total Fixed Expenses Page 2			
Gas			
Propane			
Black Tank			
Grey Tank			
Water			
Food			
Laundry			
Medical			
Medication			
Repairs			
Total			

Notes

Month			**Campground List**				
Day	Campground Name	City	Cost	Rating	Cell Service	Day Limit	Comment
1							
2							
3							
4							
5							
6							
7							
8							
9							
10							
11							
12							
13							
14							
15							
16							
17							
18							
19							
20							
21							
22							
23							
24							
25							
26							
27							
28							
29							
30							
31							

Month

Monthly Income				
	Left from last month	Added	Spent	Balance
Retiredment Check				
Work Pay Check				
Youtube				
Amazon				
Etsy				
401K				
Other income 1				
Other income 2				
Other income 3				
Totals				

Fixed Expenses				
	Amount from last month	Added	Spent	Balance
Camper Payment				
Phone				
Internet				
Amazon				
Netflix				
Health Insureance				
Vehicle Insureance				
Post Office Box				
Totals				

Monthly Expenses												
Date	Gas	Propane	BlackTank	GreyTank	Water	Food	Laundry	Medical	Medication	Repairs		
1												
2												
3												
4												
5												
6												
7												
8												
9												
10												
11												
12												
13												
14												
15												
16												
17												
18												
19												
20												
21												
22												
23												
24												
25												
26												
27												
28												
29												
30												
31												
Total												

Other Monthly Expenses												
Date												
1												
2												
3												
4												
5												
6												
7												
8												
9												
10												
11												
12												
13												
14												
15												
16												
17												
18												
19												
20												
21												
22												
23												
24												
25												
26												
27												
28												
29												
30												
31												
Total												

Monthly Totals

	Balance From last month	Budgeted +/-	New Balance
Total from Campgrounds			
Total Fixed Expenses Page 1			
Total Fixed Expenses Page 2			
Gas			
Propane			
Black Tank			
Grey Tank			
Water			
Food			
Laundry			
Medical			
Medication			
Repairs			
Total			

Notes

Month		**Campground List**					
Day	Campground Name	City	Cost	Rating	Cell Service	Day Limit	Comment
1							
2							
3							
4							
5							
6							
7							
8							
9							
10							
11							
12							
13							
14							
15							
16							
17							
18							
19							
20							
21							
22							
23							
24							
25							
26							
27							
28							
29							
30							
31							

Month

Monthly Income

	Left from last month	Added	Spent	Balance
Retiredment Check				
Work Pay Check				
Youtube				
Amazon				
Etsy				
401K				
Other income 1				
Other income 2				
Other income 3				
Totals				

Fixed Expenses

	Amount from last month	Added	Spent	Balance
Camper Payment				
Phone				
Internet				
Amazon				
Netflix				
Health Insureance				
Vehicle Insureance				
Post Office Box				
Totals				

Monthly Expenses												
Date	Gas	Propane	BlackTank	GreyTank	Water	Food	Laundry	Medical	Medication	Repairs		
1												
2												
3												
4												
5												
6												
7												
8												
9												
10												
11												
12												
13												
14												
15												
16												
17												
18												
19												
20												
21												
22												
23												
24												
25												
26												
27												
28												
29												
30												
31												
Total												

Other Monthly Expenses												
Date												
1												
2												
3												
4												
5												
6												
7												
8												
9												
10												
11												
12												
13												
14												
15												
16												
17												
18												
19												
20												
21												
22												
23												
24												
25												
26												
27												
28												
29												
30												
31												
Total												

Monthly Totals

	Balance From last month	Budgeted +/-	New Balance
Total from Campgrounds			
Total Fixed Expenses Page 1			
Total Fixed Expenses Page 2			
Gas			
Propane			
Black Tank			
Grey Tank			
Water			
Food			
Laundry			
Medical			
Medication			
Repairs			
Total			

Notes

Month	**Campground List**						
Day	Campground Name	City	Cost	Rating	Cell Service	Day Limit	Comment
1							
2							
3							
4							
5							
6							
7							
8							
9							
10							
11							
12							
13							
14							
15							
16							
17							
18							
19							
20							
21							
22							
23							
24							
25							
26							
27							
28							
29							
30							
31							

Month

Monthly Income

	Left from last month	Added	Spent	Balance
Retiredment Check				
Work Pay Check				
Youtube				
Amazon				
Etsy				
401K				
Other income 1				
Other income 2				
Other income 3				
Totals				

Fixed Expenses

	Amount from last month	Added	Spent	Balance
Camper Payment				
Phone				
Internet				
Amazon				
Netflix				
Health Insureance				
Vehicle Insureance				
Post Office Box				
Totals				

Monthly Expenses												
Date	Gas	Propane	BlackTank	GreyTank	Water	Food	Laundry	Medical	Medication	Repairs		
1												
2												
3												
4												
5												
6												
7												
8												
9												
10												
11												
12												
13												
14												
15												
16												
17												
18												
19												
20												
21												
22												
23												
24												
25												
26												
27												
28												
29												
30												
31												
Total												

Other Monthly Expenses													
Date													
1													
2													
3													
4													
5													
6													
7													
8													
9													
10													
11													
12													
13													
14													
15													
16													
17													
18													
19													
20													
21													
22													
23													
24													
25													
26													
27													
28													
29													
30													
31													
Total													

Monthly Totals

	Balance From last month	Budgeted +/-	New Balance
Total from Campgrounds			
Total Fixed Expenses Page 1			
Total Fixed Expenses Page 2			
Gas			
Propane			
Black Tank			
Grey Tank			
Water			
Food			
Laundry			
Medical			
Medication			
Repairs			
Total			

Notes

Month		**Campground List**						
Day	Campground Name	City	Cost	Rating	Cell Service	Day Limit	Comment
1							
2							
3							
4							
5							
6							
7							
8							
9							
10							
11							
12							
13							
14							
15							
16							
17							
18							
19							
20							
21							
22							
23							
24							
25							
26							
27							
28							
29							
30							
31							

Month

Monthly Income

	Left from last month	Added	Spent	Balance
Retiredment Check				
Work Pay Check				
Youtube				
Amazon				
Etsy				
401K				
Other income 1				
Other income 2				
Other income 3				
Totals				

Fixed Expenses

	Amount from last month	Added	Spent	Balance
Camper Payment				
Phone				
Internet				
Amazon				
Netflix				
Health Insureance				
Vehicle Insureance				
Post Office Box				
Totals				

Date	Gas	Propane	BlackTank	GreyTank	Water	Food	Laundry	Medical	Medication	Repairs		
Monthly Expenses												
1												
2												
3												
4												
5												
6												
7												
8												
9												
10												
11												
12												
13												
14												
15												
16												
17												
18												
19												
20												
21												
22												
23												
24												
25												
26												
27												
28												
29												
30												
31												
Total												

Other Monthly Expenses												
Date												
1												
2												
3												
4												
5												
6												
7												
8												
9												
10												
11												
12												
13												
14												
15												
16												
17												
18												
19												
20												
21												
22												
23												
24												
25												
26												
27												
28												
29												
30												
31												
Total												

Monthly Totals

	Balance From last month	Budgeted +/-	New Balance
Total from Campgrounds			
Total Fixed Expenses Page 1			
Total Fixed Expenses Page 2			
Gas			
Propane			
Black Tank			
Grey Tank			
Water			
Food			
Laundry			
Medical			
Medication			
Repairs			
Total			

Notes

Month			**Campground List**				
Day	Campground Name	City	Cost	Rating	Cell Service	Day Limit	Comment
1							
2							
3							
4							
5							
6							
7							
8							
9							
10							
11							
12							
13							
14							
15							
16							
17							
18							
19							
20							
21							
22							
23							
24							
25							
26							
27							
28							
29							
30							
31							

Month

Monthly Income

	Left from last month	Added	Spent	Balance
Retiredment Check				
Work Pay Check				
Youtube				
Amazon				
Etsy				
401K				
Other income 1				
Other income 2				
Other income 3				
Totals				

Fixed Expenses

	Amount from last month	Added	Spent	Balance
Camper Payment				
Phone				
Internet				
Amazon				
Netflix				
Health Insureance				
Vehicle Insureance				
Post Office Box				
Totals				

Date	Gas	Propane	BlackTank	GreyTank	Water	Food	Laundry	Medical	Medication	Repairs		
1												
2												
3												
4												
5												
6												
7												
8												
9												
10												
11												
12												
13												
14												
15												
16												
17												
18												
19												
20												
21												
22												
23												
24												
25												
26												
27												
28												
29												
30												
31												
Total												

Other Monthly Expenses												
Date												
1												
2												
3												
4												
5												
6												
7												
8												
9												
10												
11												
12												
13												
14												
15												
16												
17												
18												
19												
20												
21												
22												
23												
24												
25												
26												
27												
28												
29												
30												
31												
Total												

Monthly Totals

	Balance From last month	Budgeted +/-	New Balance
Total from Campgrounds			
Total Fixed Expenses Page 1			
Total Fixed Expenses Page 2			
Gas			
Propane			
Black Tank			
Grey Tank			
Water			
Food			
Laundry			
Medical			
Medication			
Repairs			
Total			

Notes

Month	**Campground List**						
Day	Campground Name	City	Cost	Rating	Cell Service	Day Limit	Comment
1							
2							
3							
4							
5							
6							
7							
8							
9							
10							
11							
12							
13							
14							
15							
16							
17							
18							
19							
20							
21							
22							
23							
24							
25							
26							
27							
28							
29							
30							
31							

Month

Monthly Income				
	Left from last month	Added	Spent	Balance
Retiredment Check				
Work Pay Check				
Youtube				
Amazon				
Etsy				
401K				
Other income 1				
Other income 2				
Other income 3				
Totals				

Fixed Expenses				
	Amount from last month	Added	Spent	Balance
Camper Payment				
Phone				
Internet				
Amazon				
Netflix				
Health Insureance				
Vehicle Insureance				
Post Office Box				
Totals				

Date	Gas	Propane	BlackTank	GreyTank	Water	Food	Laundry	Medical	Medication	Repairs		
Monthly Expenses												
1												
2												
3												
4												
5												
6												
7												
8												
9												
10												
11												
12												
13												
14												
15												
16												
17												
18												
19												
20												
21												
22												
23												
24												
25												
26												
27												
28												
29												
30												
31												
Total												

Other Monthly Expenses												
Date												
1												
2												
3												
4												
5												
6												
7												
8												
9												
10												
11												
12												
13												
14												
15												
16												
17												
18												
19												
20												
21												
22												
23												
24												
25												
26												
27												
28												
29												
30												
31												
Total												

Monthly Totals

	Balance From last month	Budgeted +/-	New Balance
Total from Campgrounds			
Total Fixed Expenses Page 1			
Total Fixed Expenses Page 2			
Gas			
Propane			
Black Tank			
Grey Tank			
Water			
Food			
Laundry			
Medical			
Medication			
Repairs			
Total			

Notes

Month	**Campground List**						
Day	Campground Name	City	Cost	Rating	Cell Service	Day Limit	Comment
1							
2							
3							
4							
5							
6							
7							
8							
9							
10							
11							
12							
13							
14							
15							
16							
17							
18							
19							
20							
21							
22							
23							
24							
25							
26							
27							
28							
29							
30							
31							

Month

Monthly Income

	Left from last month	Added	Spent	Balance
Retiredment Check				
Work Pay Check				
Youtube				
Amazon				
Etsy				
401K				
Other income 1				
Other income 2				
Other income 3				
Totals				

Fixed Expenses

	Amount from last month	Added	Spent	Balance
Camper Payment				
Phone				
Internet				
Amazon				
Netflix				
Health Insureance				
Vehicle Insureance				
Post Office Box				
Totals				

Monthly Expenses											
Date	Gas	Propane	BlackTank	GreyTank	Water	Food	Laundry	Medical	Medication	Repairs		
1												
2												
3												
4												
5												
6												
7												
8												
9												
10												
11												
12												
13												
14												
15												
16												
17												
18												
19												
20												
21												
22												
23												
24												
25												
26												
27												
28												
29												
30												
31												
Total												

Other Monthly Expenses												
Date												
1												
2												
3												
4												
5												
6												
7												
8												
9												
10												
11												
12												
13												
14												
15												
16												
17												
18												
19												
20												
21												
22												
23												
24												
25												
26												
27												
28												
29												
30												
31												
Total												

Monthly Totals

	Balance From last month	Budgeted +/-	New Balance
Total from Campgrounds			
Total Fixed Expenses Page 1			
Total Fixed Expenses Page 2			
Gas			
Propane			
Black Tank			
Grey Tank			
Water			
Food			
Laundry			
Medical			
Medication			
Repairs			
Total			

Notes

Month	**Campground List**						
Day	Campground Name	City	Cost	Rating	Cell Service	Day Limit	Comment
1							
2							
3							
4							
5							
6							
7							
8							
9							
10							
11							
12							
13							
14							
15							
16							
17							
18							
19							
20							
21							
22							
23							
24							
25							
26							
27							
28							
29							
30							
31							

Month

Monthly Income

	Left from last month	Added	Spent	Balance
Retiredment Check				
Work Pay Check				
Youtube				
Amazon				
Etsy				
401K				
Other income 1				
Other income 2				
Other income 3				
Totals				

Fixed Expenses

	Amount from last month	Added	Spent	Balance
Camper Payment				
Phone				
Internet				
Amazon				
Netflix				
Health Insureance				
Vehicle Insureance				
Post Office Box				
Totals				

Monthly Expenses											
Date	Gas	Propane	BlackTank	GreyTank	Water	Food	Laundry	Medical	Medication	Repairs		
1												
2												
3												
4												
5												
6												
7												
8												
9												
10												
11												
12												
13												
14												
15												
16												
17												
18												
19												
20												
21												
22												
23												
24												
25												
26												
27												
28												
29												
30												
31												
Total												

Other Monthly Expenses												
Date												
1												
2												
3												
4												
5												
6												
7												
8												
9												
10												
11												
12												
13												
14												
15												
16												
17												
18												
19												
20												
21												
22												
23												
24												
25												
26												
27												
28												
29												
30												
31												
Total												

Monthly Totals

	Balance From last month	Budgeted +/-	New Balance
Total from Campgrounds			
Total Fixed Expenses Page 1			
Total Fixed Expenses Page 2			
Gas			
Propane			
Black Tank			
Grey Tank			
Water			
Food			
Laundry			
Medical			
Medication			
Repairs			
Total			

Notes

Month							Campground List
Day	Campground Name	City	Cost	Rating	Cell Service	Day Limit	Comment
1							
2							
3							
4							
5							
6							
7							
8							
9							
10							
11							
12							
13							
14							
15							
16							
17							
18							
19							
20							
21							
22							
23							
24							
25							
26							
27							
28							
29							
30							
31							

Month

Monthly Income

	Left from last month	Added	Spent	Balance
Retiredment Check				
Work Pay Check				
Youtube				
Amazon				
Etsy				
401K				
Other income 1				
Other income 2				
Other income 3				
Totals				

Fixed Expenses

	Amount from last month	Added	Spent	Balance
Camper Payment				
Phone				
Internet				
Amazon				
Netflix				
Health Insureance				
Vehicle Insureance				
Post Office Box				
Totals				

Date	Gas	Propane	BlackTank	GreyTank	Water	Food	Laundry	Medical	Medication	Repairs		
1												
2												
3												
4												
5												
6												
7												
8												
9												
10												
11												
12												
13												
14												
15												
16												
17												
18												
19												
20												
21												
22												
23												
24												
25												
26												
27												
28												
29												
30												
31												
Total												

Other Monthly Expenses												
Date												
1												
2												
3												
4												
5												
6												
7												
8												
9												
10												
11												
12												
13												
14												
15												
16												
17												
18												
19												
20												
21												
22												
23												
24												
25												
26												
27												
28												
29												
30												
31												
Total												

Monthly Totals

	Balance From last month	Budgeted +/-	New Balance
Total from Campgrounds			
Total Fixed Expenses Page 1			
Total Fixed Expenses Page 2			
Gas			
Propane			
Black Tank			
Grey Tank			
Water			
Food			
Laundry			
Medical			
Medication			
Repairs			
Total			

Notes

Bucket
Lists

Places I want to go.

Done/Date	Place	City/State

Done/Date	Place	City/State

Things I want to do.

Date/Done	Thing I Want To Do	Possible Place

Date/Done	Thing I Want To Do	Possible Place

Favorites
Log

Favorite Campgrounds

Campground Name	City	Cost	Cell Service	Day Limit	Comment

Campground Name	City	Cost	Cell Service	Day Limit	Comment

Favorite Place to Dump Black Water Tanks

Black Water Log			
Place	City	State	Price

Black Water Log			
Place	City	State	Price

Favorite Place to Dump Grey Water Tanks

Grey Water Log					Grey Water Log			
Place	City	State	Price		Place	City	State	Price